Sound Advice on

Mixing

by Bill Gibson

236 Georgia Street, Suite 100
Vallejo, CA 94590
(707) 554-1935

©2002 Bill Gibson

Published under license exclusively to ProAudio Press, an imprint of artistpro.com, LLC. All rights reserved. No portion of this book may be reproduced, copied, transmitted or stored in any mechanical or electronic form without the written permission of the publisher.

Publisher: Mike Lawson
Art Director: Stephen Ramirez; Editor: Patrick Runkle

Cover image courtesy Midas.

ProAudio Press is an imprint of artistpro.com, LLC
236 Georgia Street, Suite 100
Vallejo, CA 94590
(707) 554-1935

Also from ProMusic Press
Music Copyright for the New Millennium
The Mellotron Book
Electronic Music Pioneers

Also from EMBooks
The Independent Working Musician
Making the Ultimate Demo, 2nd Ed.
Remix: The Electronic Music Explosion
Making Music with Your Computer, 2nd Ed.
Anatomy of a Home Studio
The EM Guide to the Roland VS-880

Also from MixBooks
The AudioPro Home Recording Course, Volumes I, II, and III
The Art of Mixing: A Visual Guide to Recording, Engineering, and Production
The Mixing Engineer's Handbook
The Mastering Engineer's Handbook
Music Publishing: The Real Road to Music Business Success, Rev. and Exp. 5th Ed.
How to Run a Recording Session
The Professional Musician's Internet Guide
The Songwriters Guide to Collaboration, Rev. and Exp. 2nd Ed.
Critical Listening and Auditory Perception
Modular Digital Multitracks: The Power User's Guide, Rev. Ed.
Professional Microphone Techniques
Sound for Picture, 2nd Ed.
Music Producers, 2nd Ed.
Live Sound Reinforcement
Professional Sound Reinforcement Techniques
Creative Music Production: Joe Meek's Bold Techniques

Printed in Auburn Hills, MI
ISBN 1-931140-29-4

Contents

The Mixdown Process 5

Mixdown Machine. 7

Reference Tones 8

Characteristics of a Good Mix. 11

Speaker Position and Choice 18

Starting the Mix 22

The Spherical Approach to Panning. 24
and Positioning in the Mix

EQ—The Cumulative Effect. 37

The Arrangement. 40

Multiple Mixes. 44

Automation 47

Mixing Theories and Building Concepts 49

Preparing the Mixed Master for Duplication 68

Mastering 74

Conclusion 80

The Mixdown Process

During mixdown, we must draw on nearly all of the information and techniques we've gathered throughout our recording and musical experiences. Arranging, orchestrating, tuning, timing, and other musical decisions are often made along with all the technical and spatial mixing choices.

Often a song that's been labored over during the recording process is destroyed by a poor mix. It's also common for a lackluster recording job to be polished into a very punchy and exciting musical work during the mixdown process. When you have recorded great tracks and are using creative, intelligent mixing techniques, the magic happens.

If you're budgeting for a project, leave as much time as possible for mixing. In a small setup, leave two hours minimum to mix each song. It's not out of the question to spend four or five hours per tune when you begin focusing on the small details that become important in the mix, even in a 4- or 8-track studio—especially when combined with a MIDI system following time code. In the 24 plus track world, I can spend between 6 and 16 hours per song just in the mixdown process, depending on the complexity of the song and the budget.

Keep in mind that the choices you make during mixdown are nearly all subjective. There isn't a specific list of procedures that'll result in the perfect mix every time. Decisions on levels, EQ, effects, panning or any other variable in the song are subject to your musical preference, taste and experience. Each time you adjust one variable, you'll probably be affecting one of the other variables. Practice, experience and well-informed musical and technical decisions result in confident, appropriate and often very exciting and innovative mixes.

Mixdown Machine

Selecting a 2-track recorder to store your final mix on is very important. Thankfully, the cassette is fading into the sunset. Even if you're on a tight budget it's likely that you can find a very reasonable price on some type of digital recorder that will accurately record and store your mixes. I still prefer to mixdown to analog half-inch 2-track for many projects because I like the sound. However, an adequate analog 2-track recorder is very expensive, not to mention the incredible increase in media cost for half-inch tape compared to CDs, DATs or DVDs.

If you are using analog tape recorders there are some elaborate and important maintenance procedures that must be followed regularly. Heads must be cleaned and demagnetized every five to ten hours of use. Electronic settings change over the course of several hours of use. Therefore, playback adjustments must be made using specified reference tapes while record level and EQ settings are painstakingly adjusted using the same kind of tape you're recording on. The best place to look for the procedures to follow for your recorder are in the manufacturer's operation manual.

Digital recorders are much more stable and aren't limited in their basic operation by the same constraints as analog magnetic tape recorders. Maintenance is relatively minimal on a digital machine, and any adjustments or repairs are best left to factory qualified service technicians.

Reference Tones

Tone Oscillator

If your analog board has a tone oscillator, send a 1kHz tone to the stereo bus output VU meters and adjust the oscillator level for a 0VU reading. The tones produced by the oscillator are simple sine waves.

If your mixer doesn't have a built-in oscillator, purchase one at the local electronics supply store. Prices and features vary, but for this purpose, a simple and inexpensive oscillator will do fine. Simply patch the oscillator into any mixer channel, bypass the EQ section, and assign the channel to the stereo bus. Be sure the pan control is centered and, assuming the stereo bus output fader is up to normal operating range, adjust the input fader for a 0VU reading on the stereo bus output VUs.

If the output of the stereo bus is patched to the input of your mixdown recorder, and if the recorder is in record/pause or input mode, a reading should register on the mixdown recorder input meters.

If you're using an analog mixdown machine, adjust the input level of the recorder to read 0VU from the same 1kHz tone that's coming from the mixer output.

If you're using a digital mixdown recorder, like a DAT recorder, and you're connected to the analog inputs, the 0VU that's coming from the board VU meter should read -18 to -12 on the digital recorder meter. The key with any digital recorder is to get as close as possible to 0 on the digital meter at some point in the song. If you reference 0VU to -18 on the DAT meter, you'll always have plenty of headroom, but you might not be using the full resolution of the digital recording system.

Printing Tones

In the analog domain it is necessary to print reference tones. This involves recording three tones onto your stereo master: 1kHz, 10kHz and 100Hz. Record about 60 seconds of each tone at 0VU before the first song on the album. These tones are used by the duplication facility to match the EQ of your mixdown system.

Characteristics of a Good Mix

Strong and Solid, but Controlled, Lows
It's extremely important to build a mix that's distributed evenly in the lows. If the kick is boosted at 100Hz, the bass should not be boosted at 100Hz—in fact, most likely the bass should be cut at 100Hz. Always consider the ramifications of boosting or cutting the same frequency on two or more instruments. If you're limited on your mixer to simple two-band, fixed frequency cut/boost EQ, you must use good mic choice and technique along with educated EQ choices during recording of tracks.

Mids Distributed Evenly Among Various Instruments
Too much midrange results in a "honky" sound. Too few mids results in a hollow, empty sound.

Strong, Smooth Highs That Are Easy to Listen To

A mix that has one particular high frequency boosted on several instruments can take on an abrasive and irritating character. Highs must be distributed evenly.

Balanced

A mix that sounds like it's stronger on one side than the other can be distracting. A good way to check the balance of a mix is on headphones. I'll usually listen to a mix on the phones just before I print the master. Headphones are very telling when it comes to stray instruments that might distract if not placed properly.

Depth

A mix can sound OK if it's two dimensional (just left-right), but when a mix sounds three dimensional—or if the sounds seem distributed from near to far as well as left to right—it becomes much more real sounding. Reverb and delays add depth.

It's typically best to have one instrument define the near character and one instrument define the far character. A simple dry percussion instrument is usually a good choice for the closest instrument. A synth string pad or guitar part might be a good choice for the most distant sounding instrument. These choices are all dependent on the desired musical impact.

Width

A stereo mix is more interesting if there is one or two instruments defining the far left and far right boundaries. These boundaries might be far left and far right, but care must be taken to ensure that the mix sounds good in both mono and stereo. Mixes with boundaries closer in toward the center position—3:00 and 9:00 or 10:00 and 2:00—transfer very well to mono, but they aren't as fun to listen to in stereo.

Momentum

If a song maintains the same intensity and texture from start to finish, it probably won't hold the listener's interest. As a mixing engineer, you should always strive to give the song the appropriate flow. That might include starting from just one instrument and the lead vocal and building to a full orchestration with exaggerated effects, or it might include subtle changes throughout the song that are barely noticeable but add enough to maintain the listener's interest.

Consistency

A mix is only good if it sounds good on any system it's played on. Too often a mix will sound really good in the studio or on your own recording setup, but when you play the mix in your car, your living room, the club sound system, the radio or on your friend's mondo home entertainment complex, it sounds embarrassingly bad. Use near-field reference monitors to monitor most of your mix and, as a cross-check, include some larger far-field monitors and some very small radio-like monitors in your setup. Being able to check your mix on two or three sets of speakers can make the difference between good, usable mixes and bad, waste-of-time mixes.

Sounds Good in Stereo and Mono
Continually cross-reference the sound of your mix in stereo and mono. As I've mentioned several times, an instrument, sound or mix can sound great in stereo but terrible in mono. Some of the slight delay or chorus changes that make a mix sound good in mono make practically no difference to the sound of the mix in stereo.

Approaches to Mixing That I've Found Ineffective
- Quickly get all of the tracks to sound good together and then add the lead vocal

- Turn everything up and adjust until it sounds good

- Get the rhythm section sounding good first, then the filler keys and guitars, then the backing vocals, then the lead vocals

Signs of an Amateur Musical Recording

Avoid these characteristics in your mixes:
- No contrast—The same musical texture throughout the entire song.

- A frequent lack of focal point—Holes between lyrics where nothing is brought forward in the mix to hold the listener's attention. A new mixing engineer will often set up the basic rhythm section mix and then leave it completely alone throughout the tune. During the vocal passages there's a focal point, but when there's no vocal, listeners will tend to lose interest and probably fade away from your song.

- Mixes that are noisy and lacking in clarity and punch—Although a new engineer will often attribute this to bad tape or a questionable tape machine, it's usually a result of bad mixing technique.

- Mixes that sound distant and are devoid of any feeling of intimacy—This is usually the result of too much reverb or overuse of other effects. As a rule of thumb, there should always be at least one instrument in each mix that is dry; this serves as a point of reference for the listener. With at least one dry sound, the mix takes on much more of an intimate character than if everything has reverb. Remember, reverb is a tool that adds distance and space to a sound, so if every ingredient in a mix has reverb, the entire mix will sound distant.

- Inconsistency in levels—No one likes to listen to a song that all of a sudden reaches out and bites. It's fairly common for a lead vocalist to sing with subtle compassion and feeling one second and in the next breath go full blast, full volume. If the mixing engineer isn't blending the loud and soft passages in some way, the listener becomes distracted, or worse, annoyed by the blaring loud passages and nearly inaudible soft passages.

- Dull and uninteresting sounds—Learn what's considered good for your style of music and then start practicing. Practice getting the appropriate sounds for whatever style of music you're working with.

Speaker Position and Choice

When trying to control the stereo imaging and panning in a mix, the choice of monitor speakers, their placement, the quality of amplifier and listening environment become crucial. When tracking, it's important to have an accurate monitoring system, but as we reach the point of choosing levels and positions for the ingredients of a completed mix, we must be able to trust that what our monitors tell us is true and accurate.

In most home studios, near-field monitors are more dependable than far-field monitors. As a word of advice, get the best near-field monitors you can find and afford. Choose a product that's made by a well-established and respected manufacturer and has an excellent reputation for being reliable and accurate. Your ability to predict how effective or impressive your mix will be when it's played on many types of systems is very dependent on your reference monitors.

Multiple Sets of Monitors
Whenever possible, set up multiple monitors for reference. A set of far-field monitors and anything that resembles a small radio or stereo speaker help verify

the compatibility of the mix with other types of systems. Switch to these speakers occasionally to see if anything is sticking out or missing, then return to your trusted near-field monitors. Remember, it's our

Near-field Monitors

Near-field monitors are designed to be listened to with your head at one point of a one-meter equilateral triangle. The speakers should either be level with your ears or slightly above your ears (around 10°) and aiming at your ears. The fact that the speakers are close to your ears minimizes acoustic coloration of the sound; therefore, you hear a more trustworthy representation of the mix you're creating.

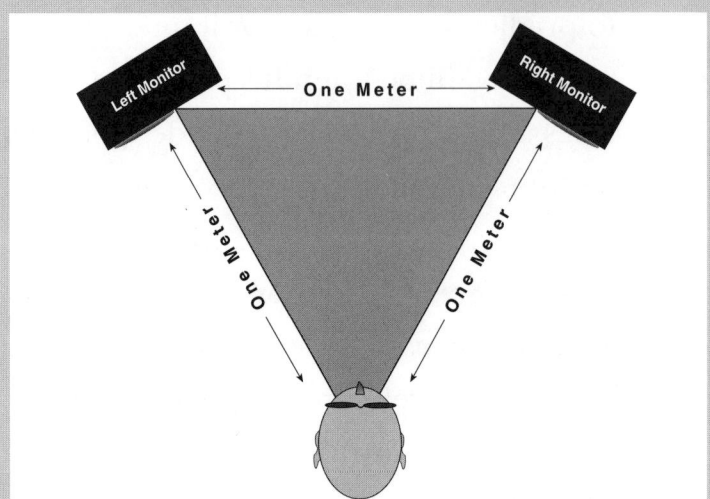

goal to produce mixes that sound good on any system they're played on.

Monitor Volume

According to the Fletcher-Munson Curve, the human ear is most efficient throughout the audible frequency spectrum at about 85dB. Purchase a decibel meter and keep track of your monitor levels.

There is great temptation, especially in certain genres, to mix at excessive levels (100dB+). My advice is to resist that temptation. Most musicians have enough opportunity to damage their hearing in live performances and it's really not necessary in the studio.

I've found excellent results in mixing at low levels between 65 and 75dB. You know that whenever you play your music for your mother or an investor, the levels will end up there anyway, so why not beat them to the punch? Once the mix sounds great at a low volume check it at

85-90dB—it must sound good at that level, too. If the artist(s) want to listen loud once you have their mix together, let them. But, take that opportunity to leave the room for a while. This approach will let you mix for hours at a time with little ear fatigue; you'll be much more consistent in the sound of your mixes; and you'll extend your career into your 60s or 70s rather than until two years from now.

Starting the Mix

- Make sure that you start each mix with your mixer in a neutral state. Switch all EQs to bypass or, if there aren't bypass switches, set all EQ to flat.

- Match 0VU out of the multitrack to 0VU on the mixer.

- Find a few commercial recordings that are well-respected and that you love for their sound quality. Use them throughout the mix to gauge the quality of your mix. Constant comparison to other recordings is a common and effective technique.

Always use the highest quality and most highly regarded tape possible for your masters, especially in the analog domain. The recording tape market is competitive so when one major manufacturer produces a newer and quieter product, the other major manufacturers release a similar product. There is a huge difference in the noise level and durability of many of the currently available products.

If you're recording to digital media like CD-R, CD-RW, Mini Disc, DVD-R or any other media-du-jour, research the manufacturer with the best reputation at the time for reliability and consistency. Believe it or not, even in the digital domain, the media can make a difference in the sound of the project. A media that's incapable of storing nearly error free data will affect the sound adversely.

The Spherical Approach to Panning and Positioning in the Mix

Think of a mix as a three-dimensional sound field. This is a very important part of the mix process. We use panning for left-right positioning. The third dimension, depth, is controlled through the application of reverb, delays and some EQ techniques.

Panning

If the wide stereo image has been created with a good 16-bit or better digital delay, the sound quality of the delayed signal should be nearly identical to the original sound. To increase the stereo effect, try equalizing the left and right side differently. Listen to the split of a simple keyboard sound in Audio Example 1. The original is panned right and the delay is panned left. On the left, 8kHz is boosted and 4kHz is cut; and on the right, 8kHz is cut while 4kHz is boosted. In this way, the difference between left and right is enhanced; the frequencies that I've selected should be well represented in nearly all monitor systems.

Audio Example 1
Equalizing the Stereo Split

Short delays are good for widening images, but they're also useful for creating more subtle changes. If short delays, below about 17ms, are combined with the original dry signal in the same pan position, the image can seem to rise or fall on the vertical plane.

Depending on the tonal character of the instrument you're recording and the accuracy of your monitors, these short delays produce different effects. On the psychoacoustic chart provided, keep track of the perceived differences you hear in Audio Examples 2 through 6. Listen to the acoustic guitar part in Audio Example 2. It starts clean and dry, then a 17ms delay is slowly added. The original guitar and the delay are both panned to the center position.

Psychoacoustic Chart

How does the image change with the addition of a short delay panned to the same position as the original sound?

Perceived	17ms	15ms	11ms	7ms	3ms
Comes from above	Audio Example One	Audio Example Two	Audio Example Three	Audio Example Four	Audio Example Five
Comes from below					
Sounds thick					
Sounds thin					
Sounds good					
Sounds bad					
Other					

Sound Advice on Mixing

17ms Delay / Audio Example 2

Audio Example 3 demonstrates the same example, this time with a 15ms delay. Notice the audible vertical position of the guitar as the delay is added. Does it rise or fall?

15ms Delay / Audio Example 3

Audio Example 4 demonstrates the same example, this time with an 11ms delay.

11ms Delay / Audio Example 4

Audio Example 5 demonstrates the same example, this time with a 7ms delay.

7ms Delay / Audio Example 5

Audio Example 6 demonstrates the same example, this time with a 3ms delay.

Audio Example 6
3ms Delay

The previous five Audio Examples are designed to provoke your thoughts on positioning and stereo imaging. When we listen with ears tuned to analyze these subtle sound differences, we're just beginning to hear the music.

Use these techniques to serve the purpose of the music. If some of these simple techniques can add to the musical power and impact and provide a clear visual image, they're serving their purpose well.

In your head, develop a global picture of each mix. Keep track of the three-dimensional positioning of each ingredient. Create a balanced visual image; it'll help you produce a mix that's easy to understand, powerful and fun to listen to.

Delay

Digital delay is an excellent tool to widen the image of a single instrument. With the original instrument sound panned to one side of the stereo spectrum and a short delay—below about 35ms—panned to the opposite side of the spectrum, the originally mono image spread across the panorama, leaving more room to hear the rest of the instruments. This technique widens the stereo image, but almost more importantly, it makes room in the mix to hear other instruments and their image in the stereo soundfield. Listen to the guitar in Audio Example 7. It starts mono in the center, then I pan it left and turn up a 17ms delay on the right.

Audio Example 7
Creating a Stereo Guitar Sound

Each time you use short delays to widen the stereo image, be sure to keep these three points in mind:

1. Always check the mix in mono to be sure the combination of the original and the delay don't combine in a way that cancels the predominate frequencies of the track.

2. If you've hard-panned the delay and the original apart in the mix, be sure that when the mix is summed to mono the instrument is still audible in the mix.

3. When choosing delay times, keep in mind that short delays—below about 11ms—usually cause the most problems when summing to mono.

Audio Example 8
Short Delays From Mono to Stereo

Sometimes, even if there's no phase problem when summing to mono, the split instrument seems to disappear when the mix goes to mono. The hard-panned split tracks are very visible in stereo, because there's nothing in the listeners' way. As soon as everything comes together in the center in mono, however, the split tracks are simply buried in the mix. The only way to avoid this situation is to avoid hard-panning tracks in the mix. The closer you keep all of the ingredients of your song to the center position, the better the mix will transfer to mono.

Global Map

Envision your mixes from a three dimensional, global perspective. Stereo imaging and panning work together to place each ingredient of your music in a specific position. Through the use of the tools available to you—delays, reverbs, etc.—you can give the image width and depth.

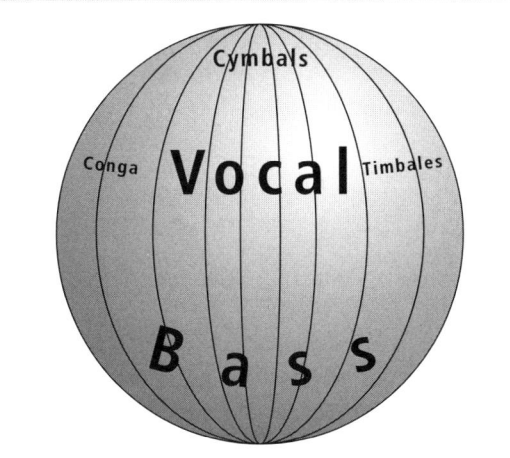

It's up to you to decide whether your music should have a huge stereo image or sound good in both mono and stereo. It is possible to get a mix that sounds huge in stereo and still great in mono, but it takes several comparisons, compromises and fine adjustments throughout the mix process. Each instrument must be deliberately placed in the mix, the spread across the stereo spectrum should be very even from hard-left to hard-right, and all stereo images must be aurally calculated and compared to provide width and fullness in stereo while maintaining visibility and clarity in mono.

Delay times above 11ms and below 35ms tend to transfer well to mono, but they still must be cross-checked and fine-tuned in both mono and stereo. Audio Example 9 demonstrates a 25ms delay that sounds pretty good in stereo. When I switch to mono, I'll fine-tune the delay time to get the best sound.

Audio Example 9
Fine-tuning the 25ms Delay for Mono

Delay times between 35ms and 50ms often sound very big and impressive in stereo, but when they are summed to mono they tend to sound roomy with a very short slapback effect. Audio Example 10 demonstrates a 50ms delay, cross-checked from stereo to mono.

Audio Example 10
Fine-tuning the 50ms Delay for Mono

In understanding the stereo image, it's helpful to realize that when these short delays are panned apart, our ears will prefer the original over the delay. A phenomenon known as the Haas effect indicates that the delay is suppressed by as much as 8 to 12dB. In other words, our hearing system is doing its best to ensure that localization is cued from the initial, direct sound wave. If we want to split an instrument in the mix and we want that instrument to sound like it's coming equally from both left and right, we have to turn the delayed signal up higher in actual level than the original. The amount depends on the amount of transient and the overall sound quality of the instrument.

Stereo to Mono Hard Split (Stereo Image)

In this stereo image, the guitars are clear and visible because they're hard panned out of the way of the rest of the instruments.

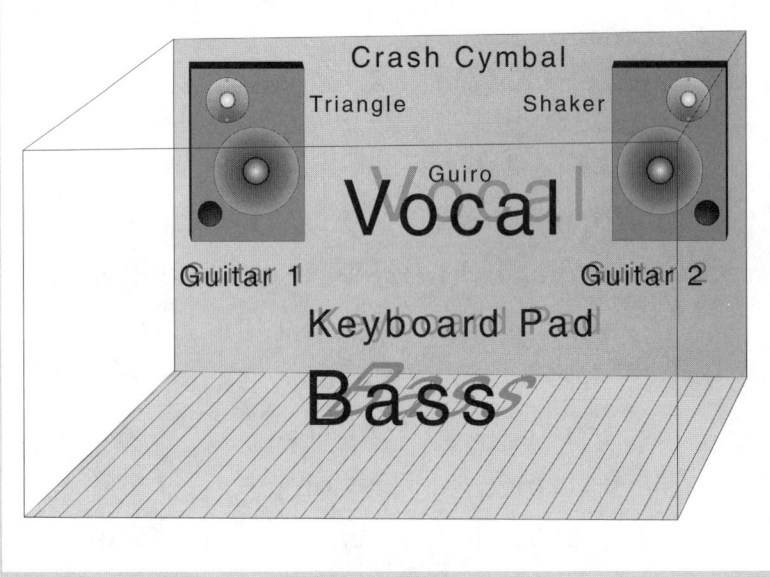

Stereo to Mono Hard Split (Mono Image)

Once the mix is summed to mono the guitars are hidden among the rest of the orchestration. The only way to minimize this situation is to avoid hard panning in the stereo mix. The closer in to the center position you keep each ingredient of the mix, the better the mix will sound in mono. You must compromise and constantly cross check your mix if you want a product that sounds good in both stereo and mono.

EQ—The Cumulative Effect

If we boost the kick drum, bass guitar and rhythm guitar by 4dB at 100Hz, they might each sound fine alone, but the cumulative effect of boosting the same frequency on all of these instruments wouldn't be good. The result is an artificially hot mix—a mix that doesn't sound as strong or loud as it should.

As an example, listen to Audio Examples 11 and 12: two mixes of the exact same instruments on the same song. In Audio Example 11, the drum, bass and rhythm guitar tracks are mixed for even volume, without the addition of equalization on any of the tracks. I've adjusted the master level of the track so the mix reads +1VU at the strongest part of the track.

Audio Example 11
No EQ on the Rhythm Section

Audio Example 12 demonstrates the same parts with each instrument boosted by 6dB at 100Hz. This might seem to sound fine on some songs or some systems, but there's definitely an adverse effect on the overall mix level and sound quality. This mix also reads +1VU at the strongest part of the track. Notice how much softer the high-frequency instruments sound, even though the mix level reads the same as the previous mix. This is because the lows are controlling the mix levels.

Audio Example 12
Boosting 100Hz on the Rhythm Section

Boosting the same frequency on different instruments has a cumulative effect on the overall mix level. We should be able to compensate for this fact in an intelligent way. The ideal procedure, when combining EQ, is to compensate for a boost in one instrument by cutting the same frequency in another instrument. For example, if the bass guitar needs a boost in the low frequencies at 100Hz, try cutting 100Hz on the kick drum. If the kick drum needs more lows, boost 60Hz and then cut 60Hz on the bass guitar. If the guitar is added to these instruments, chances are there's no need to include the lows at all. Try cutting below 150Hz on the rhythm guitar track. When we compensate for boosts in EQ by cutting at the corresponding frequency on a different instrument, we end up with mixes that sound louder at the same master mix level; we also create mixes that sound better on more systems. If we boost 100Hz on all the tracks and the mix is played back on a system that is very responsive at 100Hz, it's obvious that there will be a problem with the sound of the mix on that system.

Listen to Audio Example 13. I've set the EQ so that the instruments complement each other. Notice that this mix sounds smoother and louder than the other mixes of the same rhythm section parts, even though the master mix level still reads +1VU at the strongest part of the track.

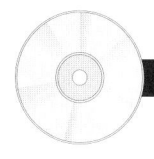

Audio Example 13
Complementing EQ

Now listen to Audio Example 14. I've edited the three different versions of the same rhythm section together; you'll hear a little of each version. Notice the difference in the volume between versions even though each version was recorded so that +1VU is the strongest reading on the track.

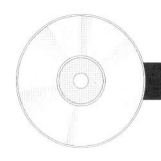

Audio Example 14
Comparison

The Arrangement

If the arrangement has been structured with the final product in mind, and if you've been disciplined enough to record only the parts that really need to be in the song, mixing is a much easier and more streamlined process. That's why arranging and production experience is so valuable to the success of a project.

There are a lot of situations when it's valid to record a few tracks that you might or might not use in the mix. Often those tracks will be turned up for just a portion of the song, at just the right time. In that context, it can be very valuable to record extra parts.

There's also definite value in planning your song out in detail before you start recording and then sticking to that plan throughout the recording process—although, of course, you must also allow for creative freedom in the heat of the recording moment.

Keep this in mind. There should always be one focal point that stands out to the listener at each point of the mix. As the mixing engineer, you must always give the listener a point of interest. This approach produces mixes that are fun and easy to listen to because they maintain interest, captivate and pull the listener through the song. Keeping a focal point normally involves many level, panning and effect changes throughout the song.

Timing is critical when adjusting levels. Developing the touch necessary to change levels and to turn tracks on and off just at the right time takes practice. Selecting when and where to make a crucial change often requires the ability to push a button, turn a knob or move a fader at a precise moment or within a very specific time period.

If you've written a complete song and you'd like to get people to listen to the whole thing, give them a mix that builds from the beginning to the end and always has one focal point. Include some exciting and possibly surprising sounds, and structure your arrangement with the goal of keeping your listener's focus on the tune.

Remember this: If you're turning channels on and off and you've simplified to the point where there's only one or two instruments in the mix, it should sound like those were the only instruments you recorded. They should sound full and interesting, and the rest of the tracks should be off so they aren't adding tape or mixer noise. Ideally, only the tracks or channels that are being heard in the mix are turned on. Even if there isn't music on a track, having it on adds to the overall noise or lack of clarity, and it can ruin the impact of your music.

Arranging During Mixdown
You might be making some radical musical changes in your mixes. Once you've critically evaluated the options, you could end up turning off everything but the acoustic guitar and the lead vocal for the just the intro or the first quarter of the song; you might leave some tracks completely out of

the song or just include them on the choruses. The options are vast.

Spend some time analyzing your rough mixes. It's very important to listen to your song with analytical ears before you begin the final mix. This could take a few hours, but it is definitely time well spent. Try to consider all options; make a list of different ideas and attempt to separate your heart from the song. If you listen as though you were hearing the song for the first time, you might come up with ideas that add a fresh, new interest to your music. One of the things that takes quite a while during mixdown is experimenting with different approaches to the music.

Multiple Mixes

Don't be afraid to try something really "out there" with your song. Go ahead and work through your ideas; print each idea to tape. I like to print as many versions of each song as I can come up with.

Sometimes you'll listen to all of your final mix versions and fall in love with the one that seemed like your least favorite in the studio. You might even end up editing parts of different versions together.

I start laying mixes to the mixdown machine as soon as each version is even close to complete. Often your "gut-level" first impressions of balance, pan and level are the most natural and will best suit the song; and printing that primal, gut-level mix frequently pays off. While you're in the middle of mixing is the time to try different things that come to mind or to simply cover your bases. It's much quicker and easier to print mixes when everything's set up than to reset later. If you have a question about whether or not the bass is too loud or soft when the mix is played on your buddy's mondo home stereo, print the song once with the bass louder and once with the bass softer. You could end up with several mixes of each song—it's common to end up with 10 or

20 or more. Chances are good that you'll be happy with one of the versions, and you'll possibly save yourself from personal embarrassment and wasted time.

The professional world is fairly consistent with the types of mixes printed to the mixed master. There are typically five versions of the one mix that seems perfect:

1. The Master Mix—This is the mix that everyone agrees is right in the studio.

2. Vocal Up—The same as the Master Mix with the lead and/or backing vocals turned up 1-2dB.

3. Vocal Down—The same as the Master Mix with the lead and/or backing vocals turned down 1-2dB.

4. The Television Mix—The same as the Master Mix with no lead vocal. This mix, often called trax, is used for T.V., live performances, or karaoke.

5. Instrumental Mix—This mix with no vocals can be used for live performances and is also handy for editing together different versions of a song.

Automation

The primary advantage to automation lies in its ability to help you shape and form a mix as you go; the computer ends up making all the moves for you. As your experience and skills progress, you'll find that automation will become a very useful and often necessary tool for producing an acceptable mix.

Automation is a means of integrating a computer system into your mixing process. In this process, you can at least record fader and mute changes into the computer's memory. After you've performed the move once, the automation system memorizes it, and from that time on, the computer performs that move for you every time the mix plays. This is a big bonus when you're building a mix. Automation gives you the ability to make new level changes while you hear the old level changes. This is like giving you several more hands to use during the mix.

Digitally, it's common for every control on the console to be fully automatable in real time throughout the song. This includes faders; mutes; pans; bus assignments; auxiliary sends; EQ; and even compression, limiting, gating and expanding. With this kind of control, your mixes can take on a completely new dimension and intellectual depth. Every move is represented by a unique binary code. The computer simply remembers all the codes and references to SMPTE, and at a specific SMPTE time the computer replays the binary code. It's a very simple premise, though it is sometimes taxing on the computer's ability to remain stable. Save often!

Mixing Theories and Building Concepts

Building the Mix
It's best to approach each mix as a separate musical work. For the most natural and believable mix, imagine the music as if it were being played by a live group. For panning, imagine where each instrument would be onstage. It's most typical in a live band to have the drums and bass in the center with the keys to one side, rhythm guitar to the other side and the lead vocals in the middle. Any instrumental solos are typically placed in the center of the mix, as if the soloist had stepped forward for the solo section. There are, of course, infinite variations of precise placement in a live performance situation and multiple instrument combinations, but imagining your recorded music as a live group will result in consistent success and believability.

Mix Approaches

Engineers and producers develop their own style for creating a great mix. Try different techniques and adjust your approach depending on musical style and considerations. The procedure I'll outline here is one that I've found works well and is common throughout the industry.

- Focus on the drums and bass first. If these ingredients are punchy, balanced and supportive, most of the work is done. This combination defines the structure and boundaries of the mix.

- Next, add the lead vocal. Start working on fitting the lead vocal together with the bass and drums. Once this combination is solid, you might be surprised at how full and complete the sound is. Many times we keep adding tracks to get a full sound when what we probably need most is to get rid of some tracks and set up a good mix.

- Then, start adding ingredients in order of importance. Once the bass, drums and lead vocal are working together, you'll find it easy to tell what the level of the primary guitar and keyboard should be; just don't ruin the punch and drive supplied by your initial mix.

- Add all the miscellaneous percussion and sound effects after everything else is up. Use only what you need. Try not to run over the lead vocals with an instrument or solo. If the lead vocal is on, you probably don't need another lead instrument fighting for the limelight. Focus as you mix. Determine what the most important thing is at each point in the song and highlight it in the mix.

Two Schools of Thought

There have traditionally been two popular approaches to mixing:

1. One school uses a full rhythm section sound and adds several different textures and small musical ideas throughout the music to add color and pizazz. There are often lots of layered keyboard textures, large vocal group sounds, and big string and brass sounds.

2. The other school uses a more basic rhythm section sound, but concentrates on optimizing each ingredient, not only from a technical and sonic standpoint, but also from a musical developmental standpoint. They'll construct the very best musical part they can for each instrument, then spend time to make sure the instrument sound is as good as it can be.

Each of these theories has its place in the musical world and can be extremely effective in the hands of experienced professionals. Both techniques can be very time consuming. When you add more and more parts to your music, each part must have its own special place and it must dove tail in with the rest of the music in a way that doesn't detract from the musical feeling and emotion. On the other hand, when you limit the number of instruments in a song, every note of every track must be crafted to help maintain momentum and musical focus throughout the entire song.

The Low End

One of the biggest concerns in a mix is how the lows fit together. If they accumulate, your mix will be muddy and boomy; in other words, it won't sound good. If you've been able to fit the pieces together well, your mix will sound full but very controlled and clean. Low frequencies are the most difficult to monitor accurately because many near-field reference monitors don't reproduce the frequencies that can cause most of the problems. In order for far-field monitors to work properly, they should be in a room that has a smooth, even frequency response.

Drums

Be sure the drums are punchy and clean. Avoid accumulation of frequencies in the lows and low mids. Cutting frequencies between 250 and 500Hz helps clean up the sound of close-miked drums. To add clarity, it's common to boost highs (around 8 – 12kH) and cut lows (below 100 –200Hz) on overhead and hi-hat mics. Be sure to pan the drum mics for a natural and believable image.

Bass

Once the drums are roughed in, we can move on and add the bass guitar. Fine-tuning the drum sounds will have to wait until the mix is further along and we can hear how the sounds are combining.

You'll need to assess the bass sound in your song. If it needs more lows, don't boost the same frequency that you boosted on the kick drum. Try boosting 150Hz on the bass if you boosted 80Hz on the kick, or vice versa. If you boosted 80Hz on the kick, you're best off to cut 80Hz on the bass, and if you boosted 150Hz on the bass you're best off to cut 150Hz on the kick. This approach results in a more controlled low end.

If you need to boost highs in the bass for clarity, find a frequency that works, but don't use a frequency that's predominant in any of the percussion instruments.

Splitting the Bass

Trying running the bass guitar through a very clean delay, panning the delay hard left and the original bass hard right. Prime delay times below about 17ms provide a wide stereo bass sound which clears out the center position for lead vocals.

Use no regeneration (feedback) and be sure to check this kind of setup in mono; it can sound wonderful in stereo and awful in mono. Adjust the delay time for an acceptable sound in mono and it will still sound good in stereo.

Keys	**Vocal**	Guitar
Bass		**Bass**
	Drums and Percussion	

Bass guitar is almost always panned center. The lows in its sound contain a lot of energy and can control the master mix level. If the bass is panned to one side, the entire mix level will be artificially hot on one side. This would be senseless, since bass frequencies are omnidirectional.

In Audio Example 15, I'll add the bass to the drums and adjust its EQ to fit with the drum sounds.

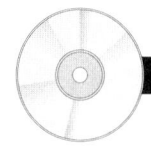

Audio Example 15
Adding the Bass

When combining the bass and drums, remember that the kick drum and bass guitar rarely have reverb, though the snare and toms often do. Also the hi-hat, shaker, overheads or tambourine hardly ever need reverb, while drum machine cymbals and some percussion instruments, like congas and some very sparse percussion parts, can benefit from the appropriate reverb sound.

Lead Vocal
The primary focal point of the mix is almost always the lead vocal. Because of this, it has to maintain a constant space in the mix. The style of the music generally determines exactly how loud the lead vocal should be in relation to the rest of

the band; once that's been determined, the relationship must remain constant.

Chances are you'll have several changes to make during the mix, and the lead vocal will probably contain many of them. Mark the tape recorder counter numbers on the lyric sheet at each verse, chorus, interlude and bridge; this will help speed things up, no matter what. As you develop a list of vocal level changes, write them on the lyric sheet next to, above or below the lyric closest to the move. Lead sheets are very convenient for keeping track of mix moves.

Compression
If the lead vocal track is very inconsistent in level, try running the track through a compressor. I suggest a fairly high compression ratio, between 7:1 and 10:1, with a fast attack time and a medium release time. Adjust the threshold for gain reduction on the loudest notes only; most of the track should show no gain reduction.

Our purpose here is to simply even out the volume of the track without extreme compression.

Vocal EQ

If you used proper mic choice and technique to record the vocals, you might not need any EQ in the mix. If you need a little, it's safest to make subtle changes. If you boost or cut dramatically, it might sound OK on your mixing setup, but you'll be increasing the chances of creating a mix that could sound bad on some sound systems.

The basic vocal sound should be full, smooth and easy to listen to. Don't create a sound that is edgy and harsh. There isn't much need for the frequencies below 100Hz, since those are covered by the rhythm section instruments, so it's usually best to roll off the lows below 100 or 150Hz—or to use a high-pass filter.

If there's a lack of clarity, try boosting slightly between 4 and 5kHz.

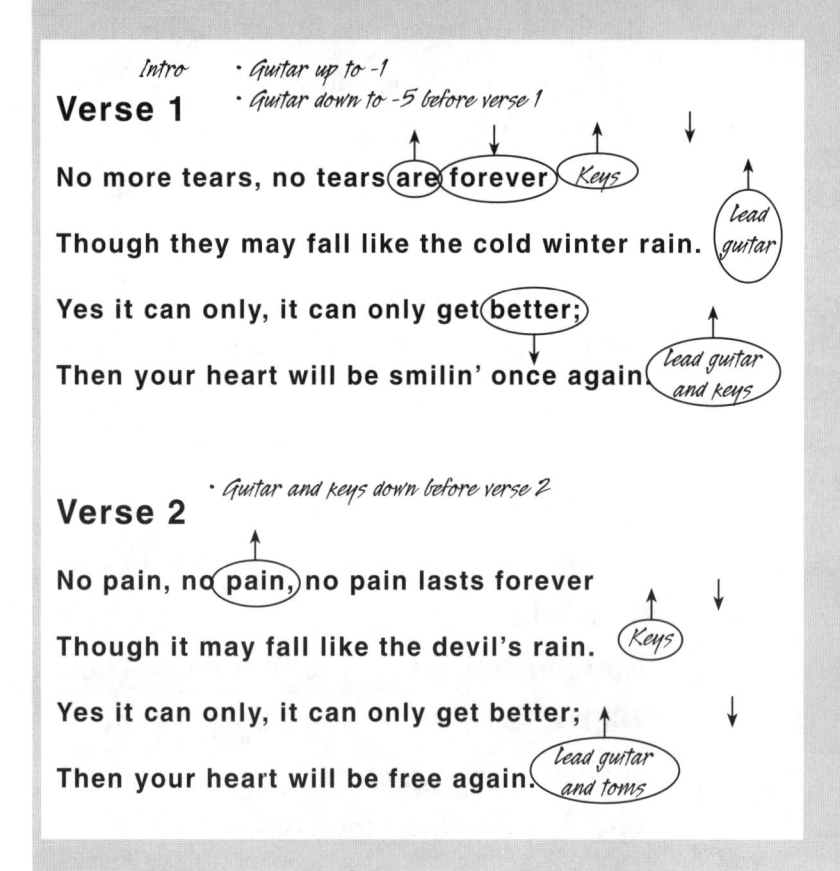

Mix Moves - The Lyric Sheet Approach

Use up and down arrows to indicate instrumental or vocal level changes; circle the change points. The lyric sheet provides a great way to follow a mix.

Intro
- *Guitar up to -1*
- *Guitar down to -5 before verse 1*

Verse 1

No more tears, no tears (are) (forever) *Keys*

lead guitar

Though they may fall like the cold winter rain.

Yes it can only, it can only get (better;)

Then your heart will be smilin' once again. *lead guitar and keys*

- *Guitar and keys down before verse 2*

Verse 2

No pain, no (pain,) no pain lasts forever

Though it may fall like the devil's rain. *(Keys)*

Yes it can only, it can only get better;

Then your heart will be free again. *lead guitar and toms*

Mix Moves - The List Approach

When mixing without automation, keep a list of each mix move referenced to couter number, channel number and control value. Keep simple notes about each move and practice moving through the list during mixdown.

Counter Number	Channel Number	Control Position	Notes
0021	5	-5	Intro Keyboards
0036	5	-9	
0036	3	ON and -1	
0048	3	+1	Fader moves on "tears"
0102	3	OFF	
0109	7	+2.5	Guitar Solo
0210	7	OFF	End of Guitar Solo
0211	3	ON	
0222	5	+1	Keyboard Fill
0224	5	-5	
0312	1 and 2	ON and -2	Backing Vocals Enter

Simple Delay

On the vocal in Audio Example 16, I'll add a single 210ms slapback delay in time with the eighth note triplet to help solidify the shuffle feel. Listen to the mix with the vocals. After a few measures, I'll add the delay. Notice how much more interesting the sound becomes. This delay is panned center with the vocal.

Audio Example 16
Simple Slapback Lead Vocal

As your equipment list grows, try setting two or three aux buses up as sends to two or three different delays. This way they'll all be available at once, and you can pick and choose what to send to which delay and in what proportion. This technique does require restraint and musical taste to keep from overusing delay, but it's a convenient way to set up. I'll set each delay to a different subdivision of the tempo; I usually use a quarter note and eighth note delay and sometimes a sixteenth note or triplet delay.

Add Backing Vocals

Background vocals often include the same kind of effect as the lead vocal but in a differing degree. Usually there's more effect on the backing vocals than the lead vocal. If the lead vocal has less reverb and delay, it'll sound closer and more intimate than the backing vocals, giving it a more prominent space in mix.

These choices are purely musical. For your songs to come across as authentic and believable, you or your producer must do some stylistic homework. Listen to some highly regarded recordings in the same style as your music.

Comping Keyboards and Rhythm Guitars

It's standard to pan the basic keyboard and guitar apart in the mix. Often, these parts work well when panned to about 3:00 and 9:00, as they are in Audio Example 17.

Audio Example 17
Keyboard and Guitar Panned Apart

Since it's typical that the guitar and keys have been recorded with effects, there's often not much to do to get these parts to sound rich and full. To enhance these or other sounds, begin to combine the techniques you've been learning.

If there's just one basic chord comping part, it's often desirable to create a stereo sound through the use of a delay, chorus or reverb.

Filling Holes With the Guitar or Keys

There's often one instrument that provides the bed—or constant pad—for the song, and another instrument that's a little less constant that can be used to fill some of the holes that might crop up.

Deciding exactly what needs to be where is one of the most important parts of the final mix. If too many things are going on at once during a song, the listener can't effectively focus on anything. Frequently, during a session, the basic tracks will be very exciting and punchy, and everyone in the studio can feel the excitement and energy. Eventually, as more and more parts are added, everyone can feel that the music's punch and energy have been buried in a sea of well-intended musical fluff. That's not very exciting.

The old standby rule of thumb continues to pertain in music: Keep it simple. The more musical parts you include, the harder it is to hear the music.

Lead Parts

It's common to include a lead instrument part; this is typically a guitar, keyboard or sax. It often runs throughout the song filling holes and, essentially, adding spice and emotion while maintaining flow and interest. If you can get the player to play only what's needed on the lead track, your mixing job is easier. Often, when the lead parts are recorded, the total scope of the song, arrangement or orchestration hasn't been defined. In this case, I'll let the lead player fill all the holes he wants, then pick and choose what to include in the mix. If you let the lead part fill all holes between the lyrics, verses or choruses, the element of surprise or contrast is lost. There's an art to finding the appropriate spots to include the lead licks; but remember, at any point of the song there only needs to be one focal point.

Lead parts are usually good to include in the intro, leading into a chorus, between verses and choruses, sometimes between lyric lines and in the repeat choruses at the end of the song.

Solos

As a note on solos, keep in mind that it's often good to put the same effects on the solo as the lead vocal. This adds continuity to the emotional flow and acoustical space of the song. Solos are almost always panned center to help keep the focus.

Fades

The majority of recordings end in a simple fade out. The fade is a good way to end a song while sustaining the energy and emotion of the choruses or end section. Sometimes an ending adds too much finality and resolve; it detracts from the continuity and flow of an entire album. Other times endings are the perfect resolution of the song, album or section of an album.

Seven to fifteen seconds is the typical range of fade lengths. If the fade is too short, the end seems even more abrupt than an actual ending. If it's too long, the continuity of an album can be lost or, if the tune is heard in a car or other noisy environment, most of the fade will be covered up, creating the feel of a huge gap between songs.

Fades should begin right after the beginning of a musical phrase and must be smooth and even throughout the length of the fade. Don't get excited toward the end and duck out too quickly; also, don't try to feather the last bit out so smoothly that the average listener won't be able to hear the last four or five seconds of the fade.

I like to time the fade so that there's an interesting fill or lick just before the end. This gives the listener the feeling that something is going on after the fade. If the listener imagines that the band keeps playing, the emotion and energy of the mix should continue even though the song is over.

If there are lyrics during the fade, try to finish the phrase just after a key lyric such as the last word of the chorus or a crucial vocal fill lick. Don't cut an idea off with the end of the fade. End between ideas.

Preparing the Mixed Master for Duplication

Editing

If you've completed mixing all ten or so songs for your album, it's time to get everything into a form that the duplication facility can work with.

If you'll be compiling all of your songs, you'll need to do some sort of editing. Editing can be performed by actually cutting the analog master with a razor blade and taping the pieces back together again or by using a computer-based digital editor. You might want to edit for these reasons:

- To put your songs in the correct order.

- To adjust spacing between songs.

- To remove a section or sections of a song. If you've recorded the "album" version of a song and end up needing a shorter, more commercial version, you could end up cutting a five-minute song down to a three-and-a-half minute song; this is quite common.

- To reuse a section at another time in the song. Sometimes one chorus section will be good and one will be bad. You could end up copying the good chorus section and using it in place of the bad one. This is also common with single phrases, lines or lyrics.

- To lengthen a song. When you've been disciplined in your recording procedures and have produced a perfect three-and-a-half minute song, someone is bound to request the "dance" mix that should be six minutes long or longer. In this case, you'll need to grab bits of your song, remix them in several different ways then reassemble the pieces into something much longer than the original piece of music.

Special effects are also possible with editing. You can achieve sounds that you can't during mixdown, like backward sections and extreme cuts.

If you're using a digital editor, time and pitch changes can be made fairly effortlessly.

Editing is very important in the professional audio world and requires a lot of practice whether you're actually cutting and splicing tape with a razor blade or using the newest digital editor.

If you've printed several mixes of your songs, you'll need to select the mix of each song that's perfect for your album, and then you'll have to decide on an order for the songs. Song order is an important part of the flow and impact of any album. With the right song order, a listener can be pulled through an entire album with ease. If the order is wrong, the listener might be lulled to sleep or end up so emotionally jostled that they're left with a bad feeling about the whole album.

Order of Songs

The actual order is often determined by the style and personality of the artist. Many albums include the third song on side one as the title song. Sometimes the title song is the first song. Sometimes the title of the album doesn't come from a song, but from the intellectual theme of the album. These are artistic choices that reflect the personality of the artist.

Adjust spacing between songs according to the energy and pace demanded by the energy of the music. A standard space between songs is four seconds. When you're dealing with fade outs, begin the four-second space from where the mix totally loses its presence, which might be sooner than the point that the last drop of music has passed. Generally, the more contrast between songs, the longer the gap between the songs.

If your project is going to be printed to CD, you have one order of songs to consider and one musical and emotional flow. If your project is going to cassette, you'll need to plan two separate sides that have their own flow, emotion and life. A very important point for the logistics of cassette duplication is the comparative lengths of side A and side B. Side A should be slightly longer than side B. If side A is longer, the cassette can be listened to completely with minimal gap between side A and side B. If there is dead space it should be at the end of side B.

Mix Versions

It's common, once the final mixdown is complete, to prepare multiple versions of certain songs.

The Album Cut is typically the full-length mix. It usually retains the most artistic integrity and contains all the ingredients as they were original inspired for the musical work.

The AM Version is the radio mix, typically edited to about three minutes, twenty seconds or so. Radio stations pay a higher rate for longer mixes and they usually want to pack as much into the listening hour as possible.

The Dance Mix is for use in the dance clubs. Go crazy and cut things together in wild and wacky ways. Keep the groove going and make it about five minutes long.

Listen to the following audio examples. The first portion of a song is edited in three different ways.

Audio Example 18
The AM Version

Audio Example 19
The Album Version

Audio Example 20
The Dance Mix

Mastering

What Is Mastering?

Mastering involves the final preparation of the musical program for duplication. Several changes in the material can be made at this stage, or, if everything is already perfect, there might be no changes. The mastering engineer listens for consistent levels from song to song. If a song or two is slightly louder or softer than the rest, levels can be matched in the mastering process.

This is also the point where global equalization might take place. If one song sounds weak in low-frequency content, for example, the mastering engineer selects the low frequency to boost, which helps the deficient song match the others in overall sound. These equalization moves typically affect the entire mix in an identical way on both channels of the stereo mix.

Limiting and compression are commonly used during mastering. A hard limiter lets the engineer add decibels to the overall mix level. If the limiter registers a 6dB reduction in gain during the mix and the levels are optimized so as to achieve a maximum signal level, the mix has been made 6dB louder in comparison to its pre-limiting status. That's typically very good, since commercial music is often compared in relation to how powerfully it's transmitted in a broadcast, dance, or environmental application. When a song is effectively louder, it is typically perceived as stronger and more appealing than the songs heard before or after it.

Listen to Audio Examples 21 through 23. The same mix is played with three different limiting levels. The first is normal, as mixed. The second demonstrates 3dB of limiting, and the third demonstrates 6dB of gain reduction. Remember that once the gain is reduced on the limited portions, the levels are brought back to optimum, where the strongest section peaks at zero on the digital meter.

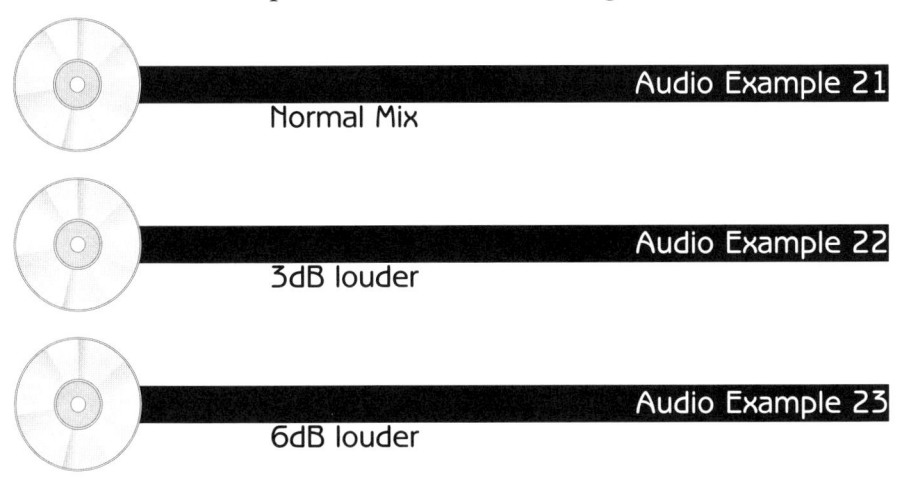

Audio Example 21
Normal Mix

Audio Example 22
3dB louder

Audio Example 23
6dB louder

The mastering engineer also takes into consideration the flow of the album. A good engineer creates a flow where the songs actually grow slightly in level. This pulls the listener more effectively through the album. If the songs grow in perceived volume throughout the album, even if it's nearly imperceptible, the listener follows the musical progress from beginning to end more comfortably.

This creation of continuity and flow doesn't only include level. It might involve a bit more limiting toward the end of the album, which can make an apparently constant level sound as if it's increasing—the songs at the end will seem louder even though their peak levels are the same as that on the early songs.

Spacing between songs can also be decided during mastering. Most songs flow best with two to four seconds between them. However, there should be continuity and flow considerations that drive the decisions on spacing between songs. If a very slow song follows a very fast song, it's typically a good idea to leave a little more space after the slow song just to let the listener settle down. Sometimes it works great to fade one song directly into another.

When adjusting spacing between songs, listen to the transitions to verify how comfortably they flow. Even if you don't quite know why, you'll be able to discern much about the effectiveness of a movement from one song to the next.

To Self-Master or Not to Self-Master
With today's technology, anybody can prepare their musical product for duplication. You can send a master that will serve as the production master for your final product. You can compress, limit, equalize, effect, shorten, lengthen, space, and insert subcodes and indexes all from the comfort of your bedroom studio.

Should you do your own mastering? I believe the answer to that question is entirely subject to the goal of the project. If you're recording your best buddy's band, they just want a product they can sell at their gigs, and they're down-and-out-broke, go ahead and master the album yourself. However, do it in a way that is instructive. Research the best way to work with the equipment and software you're using. Research the art of mastering. Try different versions of your work and, above all, compare your work to the real world.

What's the advantage to sending your work out be mastered by someone else in another facility? Competitive edge! When you record music that you feel strongly about and think is competitive, you owe it to the music to get a second opinion. Mastering engineers are the recordist's link to the real world.

Conclusion

Mixing as an incredibly complex and involved skill. Most decisions are subject your own unique set of preferences, experiences and basic aptitude. The information we've just covered is very useful and provides an excellent set of considerations as you develop your own mixing style.

Music is art; if you love your mixes then it's your art. If you practice until everyone else loves your mixes, too, then that is money in your pocket! I recommend practice.

InstantPro series

Take Your Recordings to the Next Level with These 6 New Titles!

SOUND ADVICE ON COMPRESSORS, LIMITERS, EXPANDERS & GATES
Bill Gibson
When used correctly, compressors, limiters, gates, expanders and other dynamics processors are essential tools for creating recordings that sound impressive and professional. This information-packed book provides step-by-step instruction along with several excellent audio examples, all aimed at showing you how to use these important tools like a pro.
©2002, softcover with CD, $14.95
ISBN #1-931140-24-3

SOUND ADVICE ON EQUALIZERS, REVERBS & DELAYS
Bill Gibson
If you want to produce recordings that sound impressive and musical, you need this book and CD! They're filled with techniques and examples designed to help your mixes come alive. Follow step-by-step equalization guidelines for recording and mixing all popular instruments. Learn how to use reverbs and delays to set your music in a controlled, blended, and dimensional space.
©2002, softcover with CD, $14.95
ISBN #1-931140-25-1

SOUND ADVICE ON DEVELOPING YOUR HOME STUDIO
Bill Gibson
Get the most out of your home studio with this book and CD! What's the proper way to set up your gear? Does it make a difference which kind of cable you use? Will the gear you have work with the new gear you want? Where should monitors go? Should you worry about acoustics? This book has easy-to-understand answers to these questions and many more.
©2002, softcover with CD, $14.95
ISBN #1-931140-26-X

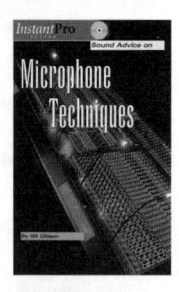

SOUND ADVICE ON MICROPHONE TECHNIQUES
Bill Gibson
Professional-sounding recordings start with a great sound source, informed microphone selection and excellent technique. Learn how the three most common microphone designs work and how to use them. Discover which microphones are recommended for different instruments and voices, and hear why on the accompanying audio CD.
©2002, softcover with CD, $14.95
ISBN #1-931140-27-8

SOUND ADVICE ON MIXING
Bill Gibson
If you want your mixes to sound great, even next to your favorite commercial release of your favorite artist, you need this book and CD! You'll learn mixing techniques and hear audio examples designed to help you create a professional-sounding mix. Avoid the pitfalls of mixing. Build a mix from the ground up, shaping each ingredient with the big picture in mind. Learn how to set up a mix that has power and impact.
©2002, softcover with CD, $14.95
1-931140-29-4

SOUND ADVICE ON MIDI PRODUCTION
Bill Gibson
Whether you're creating a MIDI sequencing extravaganza, supporting an acoustic recording, or synchronizing equipment, MIDI is likely to be involved. This book and CD will help you unlock the immense power of this essential tool. See and hear practical applications of MIDI gear: keyboards, sound modules, effect processors, recorders, mixers, triggers, and controllers.
©2002, softcover with CD, $14.95
ISBN #1-931140-28-6

---

www.artistpro.com—toll free 866 649-2665—or visit your favorite retailer.

artistpro.com, LLC
236 Georgia St., Suite 100
Vallejo, CA 94590
707 554-1935

ProAudio press

DISTRIBUTED BY
HAL•LEONARD® CORPORATION
7777 W. BLUEMOUND RD. P.O. BOX 13819 MILWAUKEE, WI 53213

ProAudio Press is an imprint of artistpro.com, LLC